D0275191

T

BEATRIX POTTER

THE STORY OF THE
CREATOR OF PETER RABBIT

ELIZABETH BUCHAN

FREDERICK WARNE

This book is dedicated to my parents

FREDERICK WARNE

Published by the Penguin Group
Penguin Books Ltd, 80 Strand, London WC2R 0RL, England
Penguin Putnam Inc., 375 Hudson Street, New York, New York 10014, USA
Penguin Books Australia Ltd, Ringwood, Victoria, Australia
Penguin Books Canada Ltd, 10 Alcorn Avenue, Toronto, Ontario, Canada M4V 3B2
Penguin Books India (P) Ltd, 11 Community Centre,
Panchsheel Park, New Delhi 110 017, India
Penguin Books (NZ) Ltd, Cnr Rosedale and Airborne Roads, Albany, Auckland, New Zealand
Penguin Books (South Africa) (Pty) Ltd, P O Box 9, Parklands 2121, South Africa

Penguin Books Ltd, Registered Offices: 80 Strand, London WC2R 0RL, England

Web site at: www.peterrabbit.com

First published by Hamish Hamilton Children's Books 1987
New edition published by Frederick Warne 1998
10 9 8 7 6 5 4 3 2

ISBN 0 7232 4427 8

Printed and bound in Singapore by Tien Wah Press (Pte)

CONTENTS

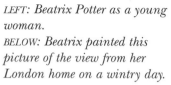

LEFT: Beatrix Potter as a young woman.
BELOW: Beatrix painted this picture of the view from her London home on a wintry day.

1

'MY UNLOVED BIRTHPLACE'

'My stories will be as immortal as those of Hans Christian Andersen,' Beatrix Potter once told a slightly astonished relation.

She was right; but even she would be surprised by quite how many people all over the world read and enjoy her books. For it is not only children who love and cherish the stories of Peter Rabbit, Mrs Tiggy-winkle, Jemima Puddle-duck and all the other animals who have become household names. Older readers, too, find themselves captivated by the magic of Beatrix Potter's beautiful illustrations and the simple directness of her prose.

In many ways, her story is a remarkable and satisfying one, because it was only quite late in life that she achieved real happiness. She was born into an age which did not encourage women to be successful or independent. From being a shy and rather lonely girl, whose sole purpose was to be a dutiful daughter to her parents, Beatrix grew into an astonishingly successful author who was able to earn money from her books. It was then that she felt able to break away from her family and do what she wanted to do: to marry the man of her choice and to live a peaceful, hard-working life as a farmer and sheep-breeder in the Lake District.

Beatrix Potter was born in 1866 and lived at No. 2, Bolton Gardens, in London—'my unloved birthplace' as she was to refer to it many years later, after it had been bombed during the Second World War. Tall and rather gloomy, the house was situated in a respectable and well-to-do area. It was the kind of house that needed a lot of work and a lot of servants to keep it in order.

Mr and Mrs Potter were wealthy. Both their families had made money in cotton production in the North of England—an ancestry of which Beatrix was very proud. All her life, she was to admire the tough, level-headed practicality of the

Northerner. Rupert Potter, her father, had no need to work, although he was a qualified barrister. He and his wife lived a life of leisured and comfortable ease.

In many ways they took a great deal of trouble with Beatrix and her brother, Bertram, who was six years younger. But like many Victorians, Mr and Mrs Potter

simply did not consider altering their habits to suit their children. After all, Beatrix had a clean, starched frock every morning and 'cotton stockings

ABOVE: Beatrix's father, Rupert Potter, in his lawyer's wig.
LEFT: Helen Potter, Beatrix's mother.
OPPOSITE: Beatrix aged about four, with William Gaskell.

striped round and round like a zebra's legs'. She had a black wooden doll, and every afternoon Beatrix was taken for a walk by a nursemaid in the park. She was well looked after, compared to many children who lived in terrible poverty not far from Bolton Gardens.

Beatrix and Bertram became great companions and shared many interests, in particular, a fascination with animals. When he was old enough Bertram was sent away to school, leaving Beatrix on her own. Mr Potter had a circle of political and artistic friends and acquaintances, so Beatrix grew up knowing interesting and varied adult company. She was particularly fond of Mr Gaskell whose wife, Mrs Gaskell, was the well-known novelist. Beatrix once knitted a scarf for him. She got to know John Bright, the

politician, and John Everett Millais, the painter who painted the famous picture of 'Bubbles', and she often visited his studio. Friends of her own age, however, were definitely not encouraged because Mrs Potter had a fear of germs!

As a result, Beatrix was never allowed the opportunity to develop any really special friendships— the kind where you can share secrets and loyally stick together. This is reflected in the sad, rather wistful note that sometimes creeps into her secret diary, which she began writing in code when she was fifteen. Nor was this lack of friendship compensated for by a truly intimate and loving relationship with her parents. She was fond of them, and of her father in particular. As she grew older a companionship developed between the two, but with Helen Potter, her mother, she was always to maintain a distance.

Beatrix, then, had to rely on her own resources from a very early age for her amusement. She was a rather unusual child with a strong vein of practical common sense and artistic gifts. Self-reliance came naturally to her.

Like many girls of her time and class, she was not sent to school. Instead she was taught by governesses. 'Thank goodness . . .' she once reflected, 'I was never sent to school . . . it would have rubbed off some of the originality.'

At first a Miss Hammond supervised her reading, writing and arithmetic. 'There is no general word to express the feelings I have always entertained towards arithmetic,' said Beatrix. Later when Miss Hammond left, the Potters employed Annie Carter who was only three years older than her pupil. They got on very well and when Annie departed to get married and live in Wandsworth, Beatrix kept in close touch with her and her eight children. These children were to play an important part in Beatrix's life.

The long hours of solitude that stretched out between lessons and seeing her parents, gave Beatrix the chance to create her own special and absorbing world. She had a gift for really looking at things and she was a born artist. Her father, who had a great interest in painting and drawing, encouraged her in this pursuit. From a very early age, she produced excellent work. Her subjects were mostly animals, insects and plants—the things that fascinated her—all drawn and painted with remarkable skill and sensitivity.

OPPOSITE:Beatrix with her brother Bertram.
RIGHT: A page of caterpillars from the sketchbook Beatrix kept when she was nine years old.

ABOVE: A corner of the schoolroom at Bolton Gardens, drawn by Beatrix. This is where Beatrix and Bertram kept their pets. A birdcage can be seen by the fireplace and a tortoise is on the rug in front of the fire.

There is a delightful study of caterpillars which she did when she was only nine, and another of a rabbit, done in 1880 when she was fourteen.

Then there was the private zoo. Whenever they had a chance, she and Bertram would collect beetles, caterpillars, mice, frogs, hedgehogs, lizards, bats—anything! These would be smuggled up to the children's rooms, and long hours were then spent watching and recording the animals' and insects' habits. Beatrix and Bertram even took the dead bodies of some animals and boiled them because they wanted to study the skeletons. There was always something interesting to think about, and many of their animals became well-loved pets.

Each Easter, the Potter family left London for a month. Usually they would stay at a seaside resort on the South Coast, or at Camfield Place in Hertfordshire, the home of Beatrix's grandmother. In the summer, the holiday was extended to three months, and from the age of five until she was fifteen, Beatrix stayed at Dalguise House in Perthshire. After that, Dalguise was no longer for hire and the Potters took their holiday in the Lake District, a part of England that Beatrix was later to immortalise in her books. It was on these visits that Beatrix grew to love the countryside with a passion.

For her, Dalguise spelt freedom and beauty. It was a wonderful 'fairyland' of wild flowers, animals, fungi, woods and streams. Except for Sundays, non-fishing days when Mr Potter and his guests took Beatrix and Bertram on long walks, the children were left to themselves. Together, they scoured the fields and hedgerows for toadstools, caterpillars, birds' eggs and snakeskins. Beatrix drew and painted to her heart's content, relishing every moment.

With each year that passed, Beatrix's feeling of 'coming home' intensified. It was among the sights and smells of the countryside, so very different from the crowds and built-up streets of the city, that the artist and writer in her was allowed to grow.

ABOVE: *A family party at Dalguise House in Scotland. Mr Potter and his friends enjoyed fishing and some of the salmon they have caught can be seen on the grass in front of Beatrix.*
OPPOSITE: *Beatrix's watercolour study of a lizard, painted from different angles.*

2

EARLY STRUGGLES

When Annie Carter left to become Mrs Moore in June 1885, Beatrix considered that at nineteen she was, at last, grown up.

She now faced the question: what was she going to do with her life? Because she was a girl, Beatrix was not expected to have a career and, if she remained unmarried, her duty would be to take care of her parents in their old age, the fate of many Victorian spinsters. Beatrix had never been given the opportunity to shine at social gatherings where she might have attracted a suitable husband. She had no real friends of her own age and often felt shy and awkward in company. In her journal there are hints that she found it all unbearably tedious and black at times. Perhaps as a result she was often ill. In 1885 she had a bad attack of rheumatic fever when much of her hair fell out, leaving her with a permanent bald patch. In 1887 she had another bout that weakened her heart.

She dealt with her fits of depression by keeping up her studies and her painting. The urge to set down on paper

ABOVE: *Beatrix aged nineteen, on holiday with her father and brother at her grandparents' house. Her hair had been cut short after her illness.*
OPPOSITE: *A page of Beatrix's code writing.*

anything that she considered beautiful was irresistible. 'I cannot rest,' she wrote. 'I must draw, however poor the result, and when I have a bad time come over me, it is a stronger desire than ever.' She spent many hours at what is now the Natural History Museum in Kensington, studying and drawing the exhibits. She learnt whole Shakespeare plays by heart, and kept up her journal written in the smallest of handwriting. Many years later, it was deciphered. Its entries reflect someone who was shrewd, practical, sometimes funny, and an interested observer of what was going on in the world.

London was not a peaceful place and Beatrix describes with relish the riots, dynamite plots, horrid murders and political agitation that she read about in the newspapers. Like her father, Beatrix took a critical interest in painting and went with him to see many exhibitions, noting her reactions in great detail. Her journal also reveals that she was an active photographer and, as she grew older, increasingly fascinated by her hobby of fossil collecting. Even stronger was her passion for the study of fungi. On holiday in August 1894 she excitedly records finding 'upwards of twenty sorts in a few minutes'. She spent hours drawing and painting the

many specimens she collected, with exquisite care.

She thought hard about fungi. She discovered a way of germinating spores and developed her own ideas about this process. Sir Henry Roscoe, her uncle, was so impressed with these ideas that in May 1896 he decided to introduce her to some of his scientific friends who worked at Kew Gardens. Sadly, his initiative came to nothing. The rather stuffy gentlemen who worked at this establishment were not willing to admit that a young girl might have something serious to offer. Beatrix did achieve one success, however, when a paper she had written was read out at a meeting of the Linnean Society, a distinguished scientific body devoted to the study of natural history. It was read for her by Mr George Massee, an official at Kew, because women were not allowed to attend the meetings.

Even so, Beatrix realised that it was not going to

be possible to immerse herself in the study of fungi. Gradually all her work was packed up into portfolios and put away.

By now, Beatrix also knew that she could not depend on Bertram for regular companionship. He seldom stayed at home for long and eventually left London altogether and went to live in Scotland, where he became a farmer. In November 1896 Beatrix bleakly records: 'We came home on October 6th. Bertram going North on the 5th.'

She still had her animals and they never failed to provide her with amusement and inspiration. Poor Miss Xarifa, her mouse, had died, as had Bertram's bat and Punch, the frog. Sammy, her pet rat, went on holiday with her, as well as her rabbit, Benjamin Bouncer. Benjamin was always much admired and petted wherever he went, so much so that he got toothache from too many peppermints. Of Peter, her other rabbit, Beatrix wrote that he was very good at tricks and that his temper was unfailingly sweet. Her hedgehog, the 'very stout short person'

OPPOSITE: Fossils from Troutbeck in the Lake District, painted by Beatrix in 1895.
RIGHT: Spike Cap fungus, one of the toadstools Beatrix found on holiday in the Lake District in August 1894.

*LEFT: **Beatrix with Benjamin Bouncer on a lead.*** *OPPOSITE: **Noel Moore.***

who was later to be immortalised as Mrs Tiggy-winkle, always travelled concealed in a basket.

Beatrix had achieved one small triumph during these years. Her uncle Henry Roscoe had suggested that Beatrix might earn some money by selling her drawings. Early in 1890, with the help of her brother, she arranged to show some rabbit drawings to the firm Hildesheimer & Faulkner, who bought them there and then (for the grand sum of £6) to use as Christmas cards. Beatrix was elated. Her first act was to give Benjamin Bouncer, who had been such a faithful model, a cupful of hemp seeds.

3

THE TALE OF PETER RABBIT

Beatrix kept in touch with her ex-governess Annie Carter, now Mrs Moore, and grew very fond of her children. Whenever Mrs Potter permitted her to go, Beatrix drove over the river to peaceful Wandsworth. Her arrival was always greeted with great excitement. The carriage door would open and out Beatrix would climb, often bearing her box of white mice or her rabbit, and sometimes presents.

She got into the habit of writing to the children when she was on holiday. In September 1893 she wrote to Noel, the eldest, who was ill in bed. 'My dear Noel,' she began, 'I don't know what to write to you, so I shall tell you a story about four little rabbits whose names were—Flopsy, Mopsy, Cottontail and Peter.' The letter, sprinkled with pen and ink drawings, went on to tell the story of what was to become the most famous rabbit in the world.

Noel kept his letter; and the children were so delighted with the other letters they received describing Squirrel Nutkin, Mr Jeremy Fisher and their adventures, that they kept theirs too.

The success of her venture with Hildesheimer & Faulkner gave Beatrix's thoughts a new direction. Perhaps she could publish her stories? Seven years after she had written her first picture letter to Noel, she asked to borrow it back and set about turning it into publishable form. In a small exercise book she wrote out her words on one page, and on the opposite page stuck in pen and ink drawings. A coloured illustration was included as a frontispiece.

With the help of her good friend Canon Rawnsley, whom she had met on one of the family holidays in the Lake District, Beatrix sent off her manuscript to six publishers. Back came six rejections—a daunting experience for any would-be author.

Characteristically, Beatrix did not give up. She decided

The Tale of
PETER RABBIT.

By BEATRIX POTTER.

COPYRIGHT.

LEFT: Beatrix's privately-printed edition of The Tale of Peter Rabbit.
BELOW: The first commercial edition of The Tale of Peter Rabbit, *published in 1902.*

OPPOSITE: The Peter Rabbit picture letter that Beatrix wrote to Noel Moore.

THE TALE OF
PETER RABBIT

BY
BEATRIX POTTER
F·WARNE & Cº

instead to use some of her savings to publish the book privately. Taking advice about the right kind of printers from another friend, Beatrix arranged for 250 copies to be printed. In December 1901, *The Tale of Peter Rabbit* rolled off the presses. Beatrix gave some copies away and sold the rest for 1*s.* 2*d.*(6p) each. They proved so popular that she had to have 200 more printed.

Meanwhile Canon Rawnsley had sent another version of *The Tale of Peter Rabbit*, written by him in verse, to a publishing firm called Frederick Warne & Co. They liked the drawings but not the verses! Would Miss Potter consider turning her black and white drawings into coloured ones, and was she prepared to turn the verses into prose?

Beatrix agreed to their requests. Using her privately printed edition as her guide, she entered wholeheartedly into the negotiations that followed.

From the beginning she displayed an excellent grasp of the technicalities of publishing a book and, surprisingly for someone who had had rather a sheltered upbringing, a good business sense. She wanted the book to be small enough for children's hands to hold comfortably. She wanted it to be cheap. She had views on the colour of the cloth binding, on the quality of the illustrations and was very particular about the exact wording of her story. As a result, Frederick Warne found they were dealing with a politely determined author who knew exactly what she wanted.

Her instincts were correct. The small, beautifully produced, inexpensive books that became her trademark hit just the right note with parents and children. *The Tale of Peter Rabbit* was published by Warne in 1902. By the end of 1903 it had sold 50,000 copies. Beatrix Potter, the author, was launched.

4

SUCCESS WITH WRITING

Once started on this new venture, Beatrix found the ideas came thick and fast. 'I was cram full of stories,' she later wrote. The publication of *The Tale of Peter Rabbit* had unlocked the door to her creative impulses and had given her the key to an enchanted world.

Beatrix wasn't sure if Warne wanted a second book quite so soon after the first. She was concerned that they might cut out some of her favourite rhymes in the text, so decided to get *The Tailor of Gloucester* privately printed.

She had developed the idea for the story when she was on one of several successful holidays with a cousin, Caroline Hutton, near the city of Gloucester. The original visit in 1894 had been a momentous one. For the first time, at the age of twenty-eight, Beatrix was given permission by her parents to travel on the train alone. The prospect had been almost too much for her and she had developed a sick headache. Luckily Caroline, who was made of sterner stuff, had been on hand to carry her off.

In Gloucester, Beatrix was told this story: a tailor had been asked to make a very special waistcoat for the mayor to wear at an important occasion, but by Saturday night it was still incomplete. The tailor had gone home very worried, only to return to his shop on Monday morning to find that his waistcoat was finished, except for one buttonhole. Pinned onto it was a little note which read, 'No more twist'. The explanation? His two assistants had crept secretly into the shop and sewn away all Sunday to help out their master.

Beatrix was delighted by this story and, there and then,

ABOVE: Beatrix sketched the son of the family coachman posing for the tailor of Gloucester.
LEFT: The book illustration showing the tailor sitting cross-legged on his work table.
OPPOSITE: Little mice sewing by candlelight in The Tailor of Gloucester.

sat down in Gloucester to sketch some scenes for the book that was forming in her mind. Back in London, she set to work properly, visiting a tailor's shop in Chelsea for some first-hand research.

Her version of the tailor's story was to be a little different. She decided that it was the mice who helped the

28

tailor and she used her two pet mice, Hunca Munca and Tom Thumb, as models for the pictures.

By December 1901 the story was written into a stiffly covered exercise book and she included many old nursery rhymes and verses. *The Tailor of Gloucester* was to become her favourite work and she often regretted that it was not more popular. Her vision of the tired tailor struggling to finish his work in the bad light of winter is particularly haunting. So, too, are her pictures of the mice sewing busily away at night, leaving behind a note with 'No more twist' written on it in the minutest of handwriting.

After Beatrix had printed her private edition, Warne decided they wished to publish it, which they did, in a slightly shorter form, in 1903. They also published in the same year, Beatrix's third book, *The Tale of Squirrel Nutkin.*

This is the story of the irrepressible Nutkin and his friends going to gather nuts on an island in Derwentwater and tangling with Old Brown, the owl. It was the first of many stories that celebrated the part of England she particularly loved. Like many of the places that appear in Beatrix's books, 'Owl Island' can still be visited today.

A pattern had been set. From now on until she married in 1913, Frederick Warne would publish two Beatrix Potter books a year (with only a few exceptions) and the demand for them would grow and grow. Her beautifully simple prose, her clever stories based on her first-hand knowledge of animals and their habits, and her exquisitely coloured pictures, immediately ensured her a very special place in children's literature.

Rupert and Helen Potter were surprised and a little alarmed by what was happening to Beatrix. Suddenly, their quiet dutiful daughter was turning into somebody different, somebody with increasing authority and somebody who was earning money. In addition, they disapproved of her friendship with the Warne family.

One of the very pleasant things that resulted from her

OPPOSITE: The Warne family on bicycles.
RIGHT: Norman Warne with his nephew,
Fred. Norman was popular with all his
nephews and nieces.

association with the firm of Frederick Warne was the introduction of Beatrix into the large, affectionate and welcoming Warne family circle. It was a new and delightful experience.

There were five surviving Warne children, Harold, Fruing and Edith, who were all married, Millie (Amelia), an unmarried daughter who became Beatrix's friend for life, and Norman. Norman and Millie still lived with their widowed mother in Bedford Square but the family kept in close contact. It was a busy household, full of children and noise.

But for Mr and Mrs Potter, the family were not socially acceptable. They considered the Warnes to be 'in trade' and they did not wish their daughter to associate too freely with them—a situation full of irony as both Mr and Mrs Potter's families had made their money 'in trade' in the not too distant past. They were concerned, also, by Beatrix's developing friendship with Norman.

From the Potters' point of view, they were right to be worried. There was a special feeling between the two. Norman was thoughtful, hard-working and sensitive. Beatrix instinctively turned to him on business. He, in return, was attracted to this unusual and interesting author.

5

A TRAGIC LOVE AFFAIR

Among the papers found after Beatrix's death was a photograph of the original Benjamin Bunny. 'A very handsome tame Belgian rabbit . . . extremely fond of hot buttered toast, he used to hurry into the drawing-room when he heard the tea-bell!' He was, of course, the inspiration for her next book, *The Tale of Benjamin Bunny.*

The story tells how Benjamin Bunny persuades Peter Rabbit to return to Mr McGregor's garden in order to get his clothes back, and how the two rabbits nearly come to grief. Mr McGregor had made off with the clothes after Peter lost them in his previous adventures in *The Tale of Peter Rabbit.* As usual, Beatrix prepared the book with great care, writing it out into a covered exercise book with the pencil sketches pasted in opposite the text.

The Tale of Benjamin Bunny was to be published at the same time as *The Tale of Two Bad Mice.* Beatrix needed a model for the doll's house in her story of Hunca Munca and Tom Thumb and their adventures. She was invited down to Fruing's house in Surbiton so that she could draw the doll's house Norman had built for his niece, Winifred. But Mrs Potter put her foot down and forbade Beatrix to go. Instead Beatrix had to work from photographs and Norman provided help by getting hold of a flaxen-haired doll for the Lucinda character and a wooden Dutch doll for Jane, the cook. He also arranged to send to Beatrix some delicious looking doll's food from a toyshop. Eventually Beatrix did manage to visit Surbiton

where she borrowed Winifred's policeman doll. All these items were faithfully reproduced in the pictures.

Her two pet mice featured as the leading characters in the story. Beatrix wrote to Norman Warne, 'Hunca Munca is very ready to play the game; I stopped her in the act of carrying a doll as large as herself up to the nest, she cannot resist anything with lace or ribbon; (she despises the dishes).'

The two books were published in 1904. Unfortunately, the real Hunca Munca died some time later from a fall.

Beatrix was inconsolable. She almost wished that her own neck had been broken, rather than Hunca Munca's. Beatrix's grief for her pet was very real, but it was also intensified by the fact that she was now plunged into an emotional crisis where she found herself torn between her feelings and her family's wishes.

During all this time, Norman and Beatrix probably had never spent more than a few moments alone together. They always addressed each other, in letters at least, as 'Miss Potter' and 'Mr Warne'. Beatrix had been forbidden to carry on her friendship with him, and this situation brought the two more closely together. Norman and Beatrix had much to share and when they did fall in love, it was serious.

During the summer of 1905, when Beatrix was about to go on holiday, Norman wrote to her and asked her to marry him. She accepted. Naturally, her parents disapproved strongly. They tried to prevent the engagement and told her not to tell anyone about it outside the two families. Beatrix agreed to say nothing but, in a rare show of defiance, insisted on wearing Norman's engagement ring.

Despite the strains at home, Beatrix hid her upset from the world. She continued working on her next book, *The Tale of Mrs Tiggy-Winkle*, and developing her ideas for *The Pie and the Patty-Pan*. Her work was her comfort. 'I do so hate finishing books,' she told Norman. 'I would like to go on with them for years.' This was true, but perhaps it was also true that the process of working on her books meant that she could spend time with Norman.

The character of Mrs Tiggy-winkle was based on old Kitty MacDonald, the twinkly and 'delightfully merry'

RIGHT: Mrs Tiggy-winkle, the hedgehog washerwoman.

washerwoman Beatrix had made friends with, and often photographed, at Dalguise. The book, she considered, would appeal mainly to little girls, and she used her own Mrs Tiggy-winkle as the model for her illustrations. It was not all plain sailing. 'As long as she can go to sleep on my knee she is delighted, but if she is propped up on end for half an hour, she first begins to yawn pathetically, and then she does bite!' In the end, Beatrix dressed up a cottonwool dummy figure in order to get the clothes drawn correctly.

Before the book was published, tragedy struck. In August 1905 Norman fell ill with a blood disorder, and within a few weeks he was dead.

His grieving family had, at least, the small consolation of being able to mourn together. Because of her promise to her parents, Beatrix had no one. It is difficult to guess what happened to her spirit in the dark days that followed. She had lost the man she loved, and with him the prospect of a happy marriage.

She also had to face the fact that she was not going to escape from Bolton Gardens or her parents just yet. The family net that closed round her was just as tight as before.

Her letters remain mostly silent on her feelings, but it is possible to trace in them from that time onwards a tougher, more practical spirit. Under this blow, the younger Beatrix vanished, and an older Beatrix emerged.

6

BUYING A FARM

Even if Beatrix could not marry Norman, there was something she could do and had wanted to do for some time. She was now earning quite a lot of money. She had also a small legacy left to her by an aunt. In the summer of 1905 she used this money to buy Hill Top Farm, Sawrey, in the Lake District. It was the answer to a growing need to put down roots in the countryside and to have somewhere which she could call her own.

From the beginning, Hill Top was to be of the utmost importance to her. It was a special house that she loved best of all of the several houses she later owned, providing a much needed source of comfort and solace. It also came to express a very private part of her personality.

There was plenty to think about. The farmhouse and the farm buildings needed attention. Animals needed to be bought and equipment installed. She reinstated the farm manager, John Cannon, and on the advice of Canon Rawnsley, she began to build up a flock of Herdwick sheep,

an old and increas-
ingly rare breed.
Soon, in a modest
way, the farm began
to prosper.

Hill Top was her
bolt-hole, a place to
which she could
escape and get over
her grief. It offered
the prospect of a life
quite different from
the one she was used
to, and one which
she discovered she
was naturally fitted
for—as a farmer.

Unfortunately,
the house was rather
small and she had to
find a way to fit her-
self and the Cannon
family into it. She
made plans to build a
new wing onto the farmhouse. She quickly discovered, too,
that she had to do battle with the rats that infested Hill
Top. She described one incident to Winifred Warne:
'There is a sort of large cupboard or closet where I do my
photographing; it is papered inside with a rather pretty
green and gold paper; and Samuel (Whiskers) had torn off
strips of paper all round the closet as high as he could

*ABOVE: Beatrix's painting, done in 1910,
of Hill Top Farm in snow at night.
OPPOSITE: Her pen-and-ink sketch of Hill
Top as it was when she first bought it.*

up like this —

I could see the marks of his
little teeth!   Every scrap
was taken away.
I wonder what in the world
he wanted it for?   I think
Anna Maria must have been
there, with him, to help.

door; and it seems to keep out
Mr & Mrs Whiskers.

My fingers are so cold I
can't draw!
    With love to you & Eveline &
(to) Baby from yrs aff.
        Beatrix Potter.

LEFT AND ABOVE: *Part of Beatrix's letter to Winifred Warne describing Samuel Whiskers' activities with the wallpaper in Hill Top.*

39

reach up . . . I wonder what in the world he wanted it for?
I think Anna Maria must have been there, with him, to
help. And I think she must have wanted to paper her best
sitting room!'

The greedy Samuel Whiskers and his wife, Anna Maria,
are the chief culprits in her story, *The Roly-Poly Pudding*
(later renamed *The Tale of Samuel Whiskers*) which was
published in 1908. It is dedicated to Beatrix's tame white
rat, Sammy, who used to travel with her in a wooden box. It
has some frightening moments in it, particularly when
poor Tom Kitten is rolled up in dough to be baked
as 'a kitten dumpling roly-poly pudding'.

Beatrix also found time to finish *The Tale of Mr Jeremy*

Fisher, a story she had worked on for several years and which Warne finally published in 1906. She produced two books in concertina form, *The Story of a Fierce Bad Rabbit* and *The Story of Miss Moppet,* for very young readers (these were later reproduced as books in 1916). Warne published *The Tale of Tom Kitten* in 1907 and *The Tale of Jemima Puddle-Duck* in the following year. The books lacked none of Beatrix Potter's special touch.

She followed these with *The Tale of the Flopsy Bunnies* and *The Tale of Ginger and Pickles* (both published in 1909). *Ginger and Pickles* caused a great deal of talk in Sawrey. Beatrix wrote to Millie Warne, 'The book has been causing amusement, it has got a good many views which can be recognized in the village which is what they like, they are all quite jealous of each other's houses and cats getting

RIGHT: *Many favourite Beatrix Potter characters are seen doing their shopping in* The Tale of Ginger and Pickles.
OPPOSITE: *Samuel Whiskers and Anna Maria attempt to make a kitten roly-poly pudding in* The Tale of Samuel Whiskers.

into the book.' It is interesting to note from their reaction that Beatrix, who had made great efforts to become involved in the small community, had obviously been accepted by the people of Sawrey.

Unfortunately, she could only get to Sawrey for brief intervals, cramming in the odd day here and there whenever she could get away. Her parents were quite happy for her to make a wise investment in land and to indulge in what they saw as a hobby. They considered, however, that her life still had to centre around them and Bolton Gardens. Beatrix resented this but bore it as best she could.

She threw herself into yet more new books. *The Tale of Mrs Tittlemouse*, the story of a very clean, tidy little woodmouse, was published in 1910. *The Tale of Timmy Tiptoes*, which deliberately included chipmunks and a black bear among its characters for the benefit of her American readers, was published in 1911.

Although Beatrix was delighted that her books were selling so well, her correspondence with Warne was less happy. After the death of Norman, Beatrix dealt mainly with his brother Harold with whom she enjoyed a reasonable working relationship. But in her letters to him there is sometimes a touch of acidity – she was not always happy with his suggestions and criticisms. The main source of friction, however, was money. The payments due to her were frequently erratic and Beatrix began to suspect that all was not well.

As she felt a considerable loyalty to the firm, she contented herself for the time being with expressing her disquiet in strong terms and in hoping for the best.

OPPOSITE: Beatrix and her mother outside Castle Cottage.

7

A PROPOSAL OF MARRIAGE

In 1909 a new and important factor entered Beatrix's life. She decided to buy a second farm in Sawrey, Castle Cottage Farm. To help her with the negotiations she used a firm of local solicitors, W. H. Heelis and Son. The person she dealt with there was William Heelis, a bachelor in his early forties.

During the many hours that they spent together, sorting out legal problems and planning improvements to Beatrix's properties, Beatrix and William got to know each other very well. They discovered they had much in

common, and their friendship was cemented by their shared love of the Lake District. Beatrix was still an attractive and intriguing woman. William was kind, courteous and unobtrusively helpful. Late in 1912, William proposed marriage and Beatrix accepted.

Once again, her love affair was not to run smoothly. There was still the problem of Mr and Mrs Potter, now older and even less inclined to let Beatrix go. They counted on her to look after them in their old age. Besides, they did not consider William Heelis good enough to be the husband of their daughter. Even at forty-six, she was not going to be released without a fight.

For Beatrix the situation held a depressingly familiar ring, and this time the stresses and strains affected her health. She succumbed during the winter of 1912–13 to an illness which affected her already weakened heart.

Her spirit, however, was not broken and she was hard at work on a book, *The Tale of Pigling Bland,* the only book that contains a hint of romance. One of its characters, Pig-wig the 'perfectly lovely little black Berkshire pig', was based on

45

ABOVE: A portrait of the author in The Tale of Pigling Bland.
BELOW: The two pigs arm-in-arm, that was not, Beatrix stressed, meant to represent her and Mr Heelis.

a small pig that Beatrix had nursed at Hill Top. In fact, 'the wee black lady pig' was a reject from the herd that Beatrix had purchased for her farm. At night, she wrapped the piglet in a blanket and put it beside her bed until the pig was big enough to fend for itself when it followed Beatrix everywhere. Like *The Tale of Mr Tod* which had been published in 1912, the book had more text and contained fewer colour pictures than her previous books. Beatrix now had far less time and inclination to spend on drawing and painting.

Some of the pictures show Hill Top Farm, and there is even one where the author has included herself. However, the picture of the two pigs arm in arm at the end of the book is not, as she said, 'a portrait of me and Mr Heelis . . . When I want to put William into a book—it will have to be some very tall thin animal.'

The question of her engagement was still very much in the air. If Mr and Mrs Potter imagined that they could squash an association they did not approve of, they were proved wrong. Beatrix was determined to marry. Strangely enough, it was her brother, Bertram, who helped her at this crucial point. He announced out of the blue that he had been secretly married for some time. His wife, Mary, was a local girl and together they had been quietly running his farm for the past eleven years. Faced with this piece of news, the Potters' opposition crumbled. On October 15, 1913, Beatrix and William were married in London.

There is a photograph taken of them on their wedding day. Beatrix is dressed in a sensible jacket and skirt with a pretty lace blouse. Her hair is scraped back but some tendrils have escaped, giving her a disarming halo. William is standing rather nervously beside her, dressed in a tweed

47

suit. Both of them are looking directly at the camera. The effect is of two people who have made up their minds and are going to stick by one another.

There was, of course, more to it than that. Nobody who knew them then, or later, doubted the very real affection that existed between the two. Beatrix once confided to her journal that she would rather remain single than marry unhappily. She considered a happy marriage, however, to be the crowning achievement of a woman's life. In marrying William Heelis, she realised this aim.

It is in character that when she did marry it was not to the fanfare of trumpets and a rustling of white silk. Her love affair, outwardly at any rate, was never dramatic or burningly passionate, but quiet and considered. She had never been a romantic—her journal reveals that. And if she still regretted the fact that she had been unable to marry Norman Warne, she does not give any sign of it in the photograph.

OPPOSITE: Beatrix Potter and William Heelis on their wedding day.

48

8

MARRIED LIFE

Beatrix adapted to married life with ease and enjoyment. From now on she referred to herself as 'Mrs William Heelis', and liked others to do so as well. Always unhappy about publicity, she took very good care to preserve her privacy. When she was older, she was positively rude to anybody who tried to pry. A process began where Beatrix Potter, the successful children's writer, slowly receded into the background, and Mrs Heelis, the energetic and dedicated farmer, took over.

Soon after the wedding, Rupert Potter died of cancer. Of her parents, her father had been closest to Beatrix. She had happy memories of their visits to art galleries and their photographic expeditions out into the countryside. The descriptions in her journal suggest that they both enjoyed each other's company, even though Beatrix was sometimes made very miserable by Mr Potter's complaints and bad temper.

She was left with her mother. The two of them had never really got on and their relationship had not improved with the years. Mrs Potter, remote, unenthusiastic and seemingly preoccupied with her endless embroidery, was not the person to appreciate Beatrix's gifts. Beatrix also failed to find a point of common interest which might have resulted in warmer feelings between the two women.

The Heelises resolved the problem of Mrs Potter by bringing her to live near them in the Lake District, and, of course, Beatrix was kept fully occupied settling her in. Mrs Potter remained there until her death.

ABOVE: Beatrix with her favourite sheepdog, Kep, in 1913.

Beatrix was even busier when the First World War broke out in August 1914. The war not only brought sorrow and hardship to many families, but it also made it difficult to run a farm when so many men were called up to fight. To make it worse, her very much loved collie, Kep, died. Kep had appeared in *The Tale of Jemima Puddle-Duck* as the wise friend who saves Jemima from 'the sandy whiskered gentleman'. Beatrix missed him very much.

She was also worried about money. Her payments from

ABOVE: *Beatrix's watercolour portrait of Kep guarding the sheep.*
OPPOSITE: *'The old woman who lived in a shoe', Beatrix's mouse version of the nursery rhyme from* Appley Dapply's Nursery Rhymes.

Warne were now in a complete mess. In desperation, she wrote to Harold's brother, Fruing Warne, 'I cannot leave this muddle to go on accumulating.' Not only did the situation offend her tidy business instincts, but she needed all the money she earned to keep the farms going.

She was right to be concerned. In April 1917 Harold Warne was arrested for fraud, and the whole future of the publishing firm was thrown into doubt.

This was a very serious state of affairs and one that affected Beatrix profoundly. Something had to be done to save the business from collapse. Despite her irritation Beatrix remained loyal to Warne and to the family, with whom she remained very friendly. She offered to help in the rescue.

The best way Beatrix could help was to produce a new

book. She had always been interested in old and traditional rhymes, and when Norman was alive she had half planned a book which illustrated a selection. The book had been laid aside when Norman died, but she now brought it out again and *Appley Dapply's Nursery Rhymes* was published in 1917. She was pleased with the result—'it makes a very pretty little book'.

She was working on *The Tale of Johnny Town-Mouse* when she received more bad news. Her brother, Bertram, died suddenly in July 1918. Beatrix had remained close to him even though they did not meet very often. They had been allies in childhood and a support to each other in adulthood. His death was a bitter blow.

Everyone turned to Beatrix to help sort out the problems left by his death, but she managed to get *The Tale of Johnny Town-Mouse* finished in time for it to be published by Christmas 1918.

A new Beatrix Potter was always something to be looked

forward to and this book was no exception. One reviewer wrote, 'Miss Potter need not worry about rivals. She has none.' And there can be few who can resist the story of dear little Timmy Willie, the country mouse, who finds himself transported from his peaceful nest in a sunny bank into the terrors of Johnny Town-mouse's home. The last lines of the book read, 'One place suits one person, another place suits another person. For my part I prefer to live in the country, like Timmy Willie.' This was certainly Beatrix's opinion.

In 1918 the war ended. Back in the quiet valleys and

BELOW: Beatrix at a country show with a prize sheep.
OPPOSITE: Beatrix's sketch of Johnny Town-mouse visiting Timmy Willie, the contented country mouse.

hills of the Lake District, people set about putting their lives in order again. Beatrix was fifty-two. She was now definitely middle-aged—a satisfying and busy middle age. She and William did not have any children, but her marriage was happy and enduring.

In one sense, her fulfilment exacted a price. It brought about a slackening in her powers as an artist and writer. Never again would she produce such a magic galaxy of stories and pictures. Her energy and powers would be focused elsewhere: looking after her farms, caring for her animals, supervising her houses, and living with William. Beatrix began to regard her publisher's requests for new books as a burden and an intrusion. 'I am utterly tired of doing them,' she wrote to Warne in 1919, 'and my eyes are wearing out.'

9

FRIENDS IN AMERICA

Beatrix did not forget her commitment to Warne, and soon after the war ended she began work on *The Tale of Jenny Crow*, a retelling of a fable from Aesop. The result, however, was a sharp exchange of letters between publisher and author, for Warne were not happy with the manuscript. 'It is not Miss Potter, it is Aesop.' Strong criticism indeed. In one of her letters Beatrix wrote tartly, 'You do not realise that I have become more—rather than less obstinate as I grow older; and that you have no lever to make use of with me;

OPPOSITE: Anne Carroll Moore in her library.
ABOVE: Gardening guinea-pigs from Beatrix's second verse collection,
Cecily Parsley's Nursery Rhymes.

beyond sympathy with you and the old firm.' With that
Warne had to be content and there were no new books for
several years.

In 1921 Beatrix made a new friend and this person was to
bring her a lot of pleasure. Anne Carroll Moore was the
Superintendent of Children's Work in the New York Public
Library. She was visiting the area and wrote to ask if she
could see Beatrix.

The meeting was a great success. Beatrix had often been
annoyed by what she saw as her English public's refusal to
take her seriously as a writer. She felt that she was only
appreciated as an illustrator but, from what Miss Moore told
her, the very reverse was true in America. There her readers
considered her to be a very fine writer indeed, and Miss
Moore was not slow to convey her appreciation and praise.

This was to be the beginning of some very happy friendships with Miss Moore and other Americans who came to visit Sawrey. There was something about the openness and generosity of their character which appealed to Beatrix and made her drop the guard she so often assumed with curious English readers. 'I always tell nice Americans to send other nice Americans along,' she said.

Her meeting with Anne Carroll Moore was especially significant because it inspired Beatrix to write another book. In 1922 *Cecily Parsley's Nursery Rhymes* was produced as a companion volume to *Appley Dapply's Nursery Rhymes*.

For Warne, however, the American connection was to prove a mixed blessing. Always anxious to prise more books out of their bestselling author, they were not pleased when

OPPOSITE AND ABOVE: Illustrations from The Fairy Caravan, *the book that Beatrix published in America.*

Beatrix agreed with an American publisher to write *The Fairy Caravan*. The story of a travelling circus invisible to humans, this book was to be published only in America in 1929. Beatrix explained that she felt *The Fairy Caravan* was too personal for her to feel comfortable about it appearing in Britain. Although it is not considered to be one of her better books, it was an immediate success in the United States. Naturally, her publisher there asked for a second book.

Beatrix drew on material she had first worked on when she was seventeen—the story of the pig in the Edward Lear rhyme *The Owl and the Pussycat* and why he went to live in the land of the Bong tree. Poor Pig Robinson is

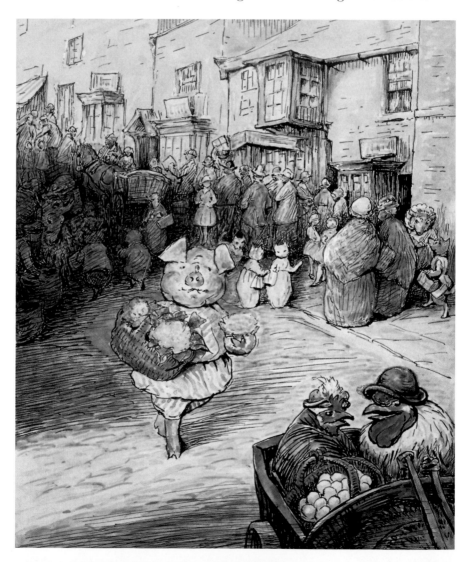

OPPOSITE AND ABOVE: The illustrations from The Tale of Little Pig Robinson *show seaside scenes that Beatrix remembered from her visits to the south-west of England when she was a young girl.*

sent out shopping by his aunts and ends up on the high seas. 'It is the most dreadful rubbish,' wrote Beatrix, but her readers were not disappointed.

This time she did not wish Warne to be excluded, and *The Tale of Little Pig Robinson* was published in September 1930 by both Warne and her American publisher.

10

LIVING IN THE COUNTRY

The Heelises were important figures in Sawrey, but they made sure that they gave as much to the village as they took from it. They entered fully into village life and worked for many different charitable concerns which were a necessary part of a community that had to rely on itself.

William played golf and bowls, and he was very fond of country dancing. Beatrix often used to accompany him to watch the revels. Together they participated in local fêtes and celebrations, and often lent one or other of their fields

BELOW: William Heelis leading a country dance set in about 1930. OPPOSITE: A Christmas card design for the Invalid Children's Aid Association.

to help out. They supported the local folk dancers and greeted Christmas carollers or Easter Pace-Eggers, (groups of villagers who went round asking for Easter eggs from their neighbours). Beatrix also derived a great deal of satisfaction from her association with the Girl Guides. She was a kind and hospitable host, allowing them to camp on her land during the school holidays.

One of her favourite charities was the Invalid Children's Aid Association which aimed to endow beds for children in hospitals. Beatrix helped to raise money with the Peter Rabbit Fund. She drew pictures for the Association's Christmas cards, and gave permission for the Peter Rabbit symbol to be used on their stamp collecting cards.

She was also a dedicated and valued supporter of the National Trust. She was generous in her financial contributions (often given anonymously) to the Trust, and in her practical encouragement of its conservation aims. The

steady growth in the use of the motor car meant that the Lake District was now easier for holiday-makers to reach, and its peace and beauty were being threatened by insensitive development. Beatrix noted the growth of this new tourist industry with a critical and fiercely protective eye. She did not like all that she saw. Over the years, she

BELOW: Troutbeck Park Farm which Beatrix bought in 1924 and which she left to the National Trust after her death.

herself had used whatever money she could spare gradually to acquire pieces of land. At first this was for her own satisfaction, but subsequently she aimed to give the land to the Trust. By 1924, when she purchased Troutbeck, a large farm with sheep flocks, she was a considerable landowner.

In 1930 a large and unspoilt area of land at Coniston came up for sale. Beatrix was very anxious that this estate should remain intact. She offered to buy it for the National Trust, who were short of money, and then sell it back to them in stages. The Trust were delighted to accept her proposal, and they asked her to manage the estate for them until they could make suitable arrangements. Beatrix accepted and proved a very able manager. She continued to act for them until she was in her seventies. 'Interesting work,' she wrote to an American friend, 'at other people's expense.'

However busy she was, Beatrix always found time to spend with her animals. There were horses, ponies, poultry and pigs on the farms. She kept rabbits and trained her beloved collies. She had a pet pig, Sally, who used to follow her around like a dog, and Tuppenny, a long-haired guinea pig, who twittered whenever he was given his dish of bread and milk. She was also devoted to her Pekinese dogs, Tzusee and Chuleh. They went everywhere with her and even slept on the bed. They were great hunters, and chased round and round like hurricanes under tables and chairs.

In her letters to friends in America she often sent wonderful little ink sketches and descriptions of her animals' antics. She obviously enjoyed them enormously although, practical farmer as she was, she also understood the necessity of releasing livestock for market day or the butcher.

Beatrix's feelings for her animals were part of the private side of her character, very different from the shrewd, practical and sometimes formidable face she presented to the world. Ulla Hyde Parker, the Danish wife of one of Beatrix's relations, was very fond of 'Cousin Beatie' as she called her. After Beatrix died, Ulla wrote a brief memoir about her and described their first meeting in 1931.

'Cousin Beatie came to greet us,' she wrote, 'a short, round little lady with a smiling rosy face and small bright blue twinkling eyes. I sensed great warmth but at the same

*RIGHT: Beatrix at Hill Top
with William's shooting
dog, Spotty.*

time great reserve, even shyness.

The two women became good friends and it was to Ulla that Beatrix showed Hill Top Farm. Although the Heelises lived at Castle Farm, Beatrix had kept Hill Top. It was here that she kept her most precious possession— all sorts of beautiful old objects— and her papers. She was very interested in old country furniture and often bought up pieces in sales to furnish her houses. The favourites were kept at Hill Top, and each piece was arranged with precise and loving care.

Beatrix often spent afternoons there alone and undisturbed. As she told Ulla, 'When Cousin Willie asked me to marry him I said yes, but I also said we cannot live here at Hill Top. We will live at Castle Cottage, as I must leave everything here as it is. So after I married I just locked the door and left.'

Ulla sensed that Hill Top was a very important part of what she called Beatrix's hidden world. The part of her that was close to nature and inspired her books, and that only very few of her friends and family ever glimpsed or understood.

11

OLD AGE

Sheep-breeding, farming, organising her land and houses, looking after her relations: Beatrix's life was a full and tiring one, but she seemed to thrive on it. Apart from one major operation and the colds and bronchitis that struck her down each winter, she remained remarkably active.

Her appearance had, perhaps, become a little eccentric. She would travel about in her chauffeur-driven car wearing bulky tweeds and men's boots, or she would walk the countryside in all weathers with an old sack flung across her shoulders. Once a tramp mistook her for a fellow tramp! But nobody who knew her, or knew of her, ever underrated her abilities as a farmer or her shrewd common sense.

The links with the old Beatrix Potter faded away. Canon Rawnsley had died in 1920 and Fruing Warne in 1928. Helen Potter finally died at a ripe old age in 1932 and with her death the memories of the shy, secretive young Beatrix disappeared into the past.

The Second World War, like the First, brought added worries and inconveniences. This time there was the bombing to worry about and endless paperwork to be done concerning the farms. The Heelises coped as they coped before, but they were now much older.

Despite everything, Beatrix was optimistic—'Freedom will survive, whatever happens to us'—if a little vexed that America was taking so long to enter into the fighting, and relieved when eventually they did. Her friends in the States

OPPOSITE: Beatrix discussing business with fellow farmers.

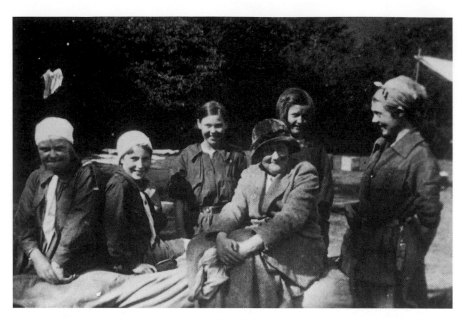

ABOVE: Beatrix with a party of Girl Guides.
OPPOSITE: Beatrix at Hill Top aged 76, with a young friend, Alison
Hart, and one of her Pekinese dogs.

did not forget her and sent welcome parcels of food,
including chocolate.

She did not neglect the Girl Guides and continued to
allow them to camp on her land whenever possible. Many
of the children were from the city and had endured terror
and destruction. They badly needed rest and country air.
Some were not getting enough to eat, but Beatrix saw to it
that they were fed and as comfortable as she could make
them—provided they behaved of course! Once she took a
party of Guides round Hill Top to see her treasures, and
she much enjoyed the impromptu sing-song that followed.

On her seventy-seventh birthday in July 1943, the Girl
Guides went to greet her at Castle Cottage dressed as

characters from her books. The costumes had been hastily thrown together from old cereal packets and blankets, but the effect was very touching. Beatrix was obviously pleased by this tribute.

It was to be her last birthday. By September she was ill again with bronchitis. She kept indoors with her Pekes in her untidy, comfortable house, surrounded by her treasures and her clutter of papers.

She died on December 22, leaving a grieving William. Her ashes were scattered somewhere in the countryside at

ABOVE: A watercolour painting by Beatrix of the Lake District scenery under snow.

Sawrey by her loyal shepherd, Tom Storey. She had wanted the exact whereabouts kept secret. Even in death, she made sure that she kept the privacy that she had prized so much.

Beatrix once wrote, "'Thank God I have the seeing eye", that is to say, as I lie in bed I can walk step by step on the fells and rough lands seeing every stone and flower and patch of bog and cotton grass where my old legs will never take me again.'

It is not fanciful to assume that when she lay dying she walked through, in her mind, all the beautiful and tranquil places that she loved and cared for. As she drifted towards death, those pictures must have soothed and given peace to the spirit of this remarkable woman.

12

THE DEBT WE OWE TO BEATRIX POTTER

Today millions of people read Beatrix Potter's books all over the world. The demand for them never diminishes. There is even an edition of *The Tale of Peter Rabbit* in Latin!

There have been books written about her—although it is only recently that the full story of her life has emerged—and books devoted to the study of her painting and the history of her writing.

Side by side with her books, a whole mini-industry

BELOW: Some of the many items of merchandise decorated with Beatrix Potter characters that have been produced since her death.

produces Beatrix Potter merchandise. You can buy Beatrix Potter painting books, linen, stationery, china, board games, calendars and wall friezes. These are all carefully checked to make sure they are of the highest quality possible.

In 1946 Hill Top was opened by the National Trust to the public, and thousands of admirers have been to see the place that symbolises the essential Beatrix Potter.

As a writer she continues to give untold pleasure, but she is also remembered as a countrywoman and farmer. In her will she left 4,000 acres of land to the National Trust to be preserved and maintained. Those who are lucky enough to benefit from this generosity, and from this far-sighted provision, will also be thankful to Beatrix Potter.

BELOW: An illustration from The Fairy Caravan.

ACKNOWLEDGEMENTS

I would like to thank Judy Taylor for allowing me to read her book *Beatrix Potter: Artist, Storyteller and Countrywoman* (1986) before publication, and for generously permitting me to make use of her original material, with particular reference to the Warne financial collapse, Beatrix Potter's relationship with the Girl Guides, and for information on Beatrix Potter's husband and brother.

All extracts from Beatrix Potter's journals and letters, and from *Cousin Beatie* by Ulla Hyde Parker, reprinted by kind permission of Frederick Warne.

The illustrations are printed by courtesy of the following: Armitt Trust, page 21; Girl Guides Association, page 70; Trustees of the Linder Collection, pages 14, 17, 36; National Art Library, Victoria & Albert Museum, pages 8, 11, 13, 18, 28 (*above*), 33 (*above*), 37, 44, 51, 52, 55, 66, 72; National Trust, pages 10, 20, 43, 54, 62; New York Public Library, page 56; Private Collections, pages 12, 16, 22, 30, 31, 38, 39, 67, 71; Robert Thrift, page 64; Frederick Warne, pages 19, 23, 24, 25, 28 (*below*), 29, 32, 33 (*below*), 35, 40, 41, 45, 46, 49, 53, 57, 58, 59, 60, 61, 63, 69, 73, 74, 75

I would also like to thank Emily Till, whose advice was much valued, Michelle Morris, Sally Floyer, Jennie Walters and Sue Twiselton.

THE ORIGINAL PETER RABBIT BOOKS ™
by Beatrix Potter

(All published by Frederick Warne & Co.)